Visual Geography Series®

TURKEY
...in Pictures

Prepared by
Stephen C. Feinstein

Lerner Publications Company
Minneapolis

Copyright © 1988 by Lerner Publications Company

All rights reserved. International copyright secured. No part of this book may be reproduced, stored in a retrieval system, or transmitted in any form or by any means—electronic, mechanical, photocopying, recording, or otherwise—without the prior written permission of the publisher, except for the inclusion of brief quotations in an acknowledged review.

Courtesy of Sarah Larson

Storks nest atop an old stone pillar.

This is an all-new edition of the Visual Geography Series. Previous editions have been published by Sterling Publishing Company, New York City, and some of the original textual information has been retained. New photographs, maps, charts, captions, and updated information have been added. The text has been entirely reset in 10/12 Century Textbook.

LIBRARY OF CONGRESS CATALOGING-IN-PUBLICATION DATA

Feinstein, Steve.
  Turkey in pictures / prepared by Steve Feinstein.
    p. cm.—(Visual geography series)
  Rev. ed. of: Turkey in pictures / by James Nach.
  Includes index.
  Summary: Text and photographs introduce the geography, history, government, people, culture, and economy of Turkey.
  ISBN 0-8225-1831-7 (lib. bdg.)
  1. Turkey. [1. Turkey.] I. Nach, James. Turkey in pictures. II. Title. III. Series: Visual geography series (Minneapolis, Minn.)
DR418.F44 1988
956.1—dc19   87-26475
                                              CIP
                                              AC

International Standard Book Number: 0-8225-1831-7
Library of Congress Card Catalog Number: 87-26475

VISUAL GEOGRAPHY SERIES®

Publisher
Harry Jonas Lerner
Associate Publisher
Nancy M. Campbell
Senior Editor
Mary M. Rodgers
Editor
Gretchen Bratvold
Illustrations Editor
Karen A. Sirvaitis
Consultants/Contributors
Stephen C. Feinstein
Dr. Ruth F. Hale
Sandra K. Davis
Designer
Jim Simondet
Cartographer
Carol F. Barrett
Indexer
Sylvia Timian
Production Manager
Richard J. Hannah

Independent Picture Service

The narrow, cobbled streets of many Turkish towns have not changed since Ottoman times.

Acknowledgments

Title page photo by Robert Fried.

Elevation contours adapted from *The Times Atlas of the World*, seventh comprehensive edition (New York: Times Books, 1985).

Turkish accent marks, which affect Turkish pronunciation, have not been used in this book.

2 3 4 5 6 7 8 9 10 97 96 95 94 93 92 91 90 89

Dressed in traditional clothing, an agile pair performs an acrobatic movement derived from a fourteenth-century war dance.

Contents

Introduction 5
1) The Land 7
    Anatolia. Thrace. Bodies of Water and Rivers. Climate. Flora and Fauna. Cities.
2) History and Government 18
    Hittites and Assyrians. Greeks and Persians. The Roman and Byzantine Empires. Turks Arrive from Turkistan. Ottoman Rule Is Established. The Shaping of the Empire. Powerful Influences. The Fall of the Janissaries. The Empire Weakens. Wars with Russia. The Young Turks. World War I. The Treaty of Sèvres and Its Aftermath. Birth of the Republic. The Era After World War II. Turkey and Cyprus. The Modern Era. The Government.
3) The People 35
    The Arts. Language and Literature. Religion. Education. Health. Food. Sports.
4) The Economy 48
    Agriculture. Mining and Fishing. Manufacturing. Unemployment. Energy and Transportation. Tourism. The Future.
Index 64

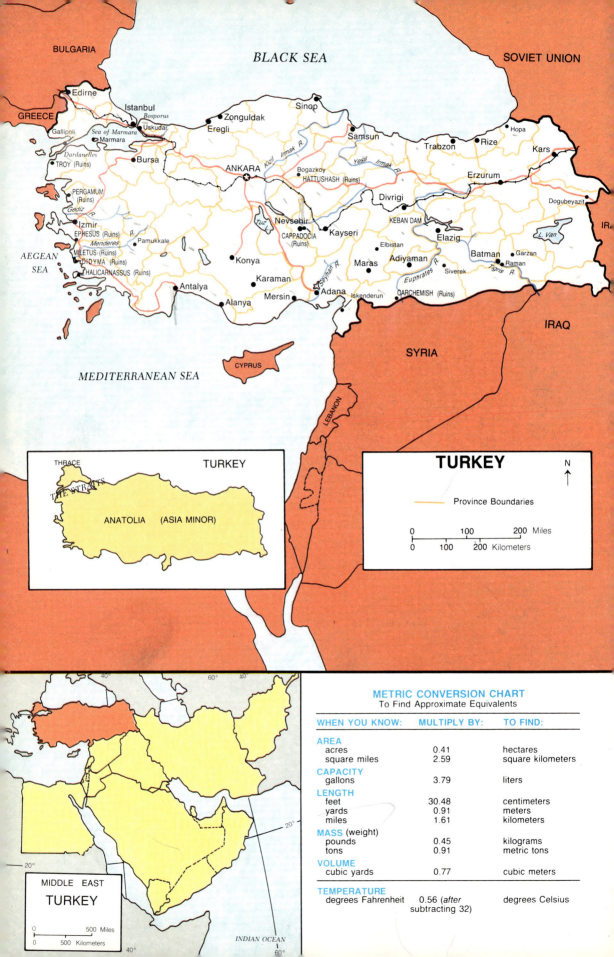

Built in the fourth century A.D., the Sumela monastery is located in northern Turkey. The building was carved from the sheer face of a 1,400-foot-high mountain and was burned by Muslim armies during the latter days of the Byzantine Empire.

Courtesy of Sarah Larson

Introduction

As a geographical bridge between Europe and Asia, Turkey has been at the crossroads of many important past civilizations. Archaeologists have found traces of the ancient Hittite Empire, which thrived almost 4,000 years ago. Ruins in western Turkey are the last evidence of Troy, the great city on the shores of the Aegean Sea that, according to tradition, resisted Greek invaders for 10 years before being tricked by the gift of a hollow horse filled with Greek soldiers. Later, the forces of the great empires of Persia and Greece marched through what is now Turkey. The city of Constantinople, founded by the Roman emperor Constantine I, remained as an architectural reminder of imperial glory long after the fall of Rome.

The people who have made the most lasting impression on Turkey, however, are the Turks. The Seljuk Turks and later the Ottoman Turks were descendants of farming peoples who came from central Asia and eventually dominated large parts of Asia, Europe, and Africa. Ottoman Turkey developed its own culture, which blended many elements from the cultures it had absorbed.

The Ottoman Empire peaked in the sixteenth century and eventually declined in the nineteenth century. From the ruins of old Turkey, a new country with a democratic form of government has arisen. Under the leadership of Mustafa Kemal Ataturk, twentieth-century Turkey has salvaged what there was of value from the Ottoman Empire, combining these remnants with the culture and technology of the West.

This attempt to modernize the nation, however, has had its pitfalls. For example, political differences of opinion have resulted in two military coups. Overpopulation, high unemployment, and low economic productivity have hampered the efforts of both past and current governments to develop the potential of the nation. Nevertheless, the Turkish people have voted to support a democratic form of government in one of the most historically rich areas of the world.

The great Ottoman architect Sinan created the Selimiye Mosque for Sultan (Turkish for king or emperor) Selim II. Completed in 1575, when the designer was 85 years old, the mosque is encircled by a huge outer courtyard from which the building's four, tall minarets are visible.

Among the cultural changes brought about by Mustafa Kemal Ataturk in the 1920s was the greater participation of women in traditionally male jobs. Here, three female pilots plot their flight plan at an aviation school in Ankara.

Courtesy of Turkish Consulate General

A view of Istanbul shows its varied architecture and its strategic location on the Straits.

1) The Land

Turkey straddles the boundary between Europe and Asia, but most of the country lies in Asia. The term for eastern Turkey is Anatolia (sometimes also called Asia Minor), a name derived from the Greek word for east. Turkey's Asian lands stretch eastward from the Straits—composed of the Bosporus, the Sea of Marmara, and the Dardanelles—to its borders with Iraq, Iran, and the Soviet Union. Turkey shares part of its southern boundary with Syria.

European Turkey, called Thrace, lies on the western side of the Straits and shares borders with Greece and Bulgaria. Although Istanbul—the largest city—hugs the European coast of the Bosporus, Thrace accounts for only 3 percent of Turkey's total area. Also forming Turkey's boundaries are the Black Sea to the north, the Aegean Sea to the west, and the Mediterranean Sea to the south. Because of its large size, Turkey has a great variety of landscapes that stretch over more than 300,000 square miles of territory, an area that is about the size of the states of Texas and Virginia combined.

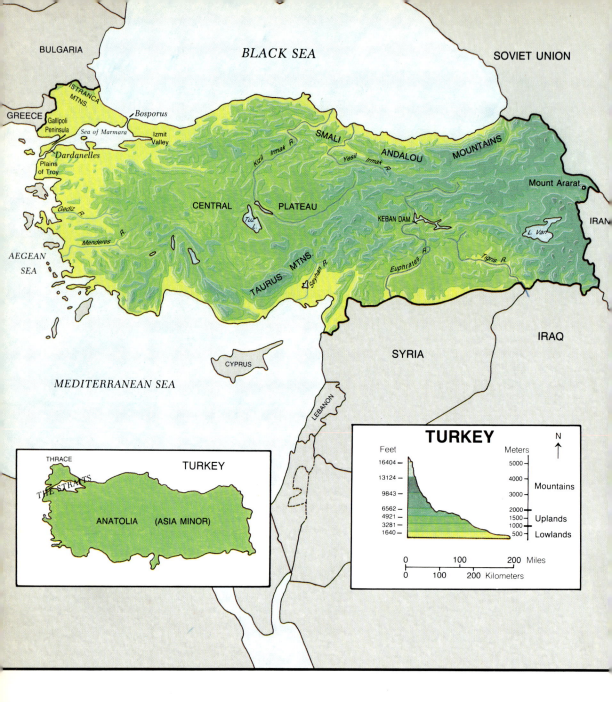

Anatolia

Anatolia is composed mostly of a large, semi-arid plateau, surrounded by mountains and steep slopes. The heartland of Anatolia, known as the Central Plateau, covers 80 percent of the land surface. It is characterized by rough, hilly terrain unsuited to large-scale agriculture but appropriate for grazing. Like the steppes (semi-arid grasslands) in the Soviet Union, the land usage of Anatolia varies. Forests are concentrated in the northeastern and northwestern regions, and small-scale farming takes place in the river valleys.

Fertile lowlands exist in the Aegean region of western Turkey. They are also found along the coast of the Black Sea between Zonguldak and Rize and along the shores of the Mediterranean Sea. The Aegean region—encircling the Sea of Marmara—is rolling country that is ideal for agriculture. About half of Turkey's farming takes place here in broad valleys, such as the Izmit Valley and the plains of Troy, which receive plenty of rain. Near the Black Sea, commercial farming thrives in a delta area that is well watered and that enjoys a mild climate. The plains of the Mediterranean have soil particularly suited to growing citrus fruits, grapes, and rice.

Mountains rising to over 10,000 feet separate the Central Plateau from the coastal lowlands. To the north, the Smali Andalou Mountains follow the southern shores of the Black Sea. The Taurus Mountains extend along the Mediterranean coast and eastward to the Syrian border. Formed from limestone, these mountains have many caves and underground streams.

To the east are higher mountains, including Mount Ararat, or Agri Dagi, which at 16,945 feet is Turkey's highest peak. Crater-lakes—the exposed cones of once-active volcanoes—are proof of recent geological activity in the region. These eastern highlands rise above lava-covered plateaus that are occasionally interrupted by basins. Sometimes, the basins contain lakes, such as Lake Van—a huge, slightly salty body of water that is about the size of the state of Rhode Island. Tuz Lake is also a salt lake and lies nearly 3,000 feet above sea level in west central Turkey.

Thrace

Thrace, Turkey's European foothold, has its own long history and has been officially part of the Republic of Turkey since 1923. A rolling plain, Thrace is bordered on the northeast by the Istranca Mountains and on the southwest by the heights of the Gallipoli Peninsula. The remaining

Courtesy of Sarah Larson

Within Anatolia's mountainous areas, narrow roads snake through the difficult terrain.

Courtesy of Cultural and Tourism Office of the Turkish Embassy

Hikers frequently climb the region near Mount Ararat, Turkey's highest peak.

boundaries lie along the Straits and the Black Sea.

Despite its small size in relation to the rest of the nation, Thrace has occupied an important position in Turkish politics and economics. Istanbul, located in the region, controls the Straits, one of the world's most important waterways for trade. In addition, fertile valleys and hillsides make Thrace a valuable part of Turkey's agricultural resources.

Bodies of Water and Rivers

Turkey has access to three very important seas. To the north is the Black Sea, which resembles an inland lake because it is surrounded by four countries: Turkey, the Soviet Union, Romania, and Bulgaria. Water routes to the Black Sea exist only from the Aegean and Mediterranean seas located to the south. During the Ottoman period, Turkey's control of the eastern Mediterranean and Aegean seas shaped trading patterns with Europe for five centuries.

The Straits join the Aegean Sea with the Black Sea and, until the invention of the airplane, were among the most strategic trade connections in the world. The northern part of the Straits is the Bosporus, a narrow, 16-mile-long channel that flows past the city of Istanbul and that ranges in width from two miles to less than a third of a mile, with a depth of up to 400 feet.

Because of its position on the Bosporus, Istanbul was able to offer a strong challenge to any hostile warships coming from the north. The Bosporus is connected with the Dardanelles via the Sea of Marmara, an inland body of water that is 125 miles in length and 60 miles wide. The Darda-

Courtesy of Turkish Consulate General

Opened on the fiftieth anniversary of the founding of the Turkish republic, the Bosporus Bridge links Anatolia with Thrace.

The Sea of Marmara and the narrow Dardanelles—seen here from the Gallipoli Peninsula—form Turkey's sea-lane to the Aegean.

nelles, sometimes called by its ancient Greek name, Hellespont, is 25 miles long, ranges from 2.5 to 4.5 miles wide, and empties into the Aegean Sea.

Two of the most important rivers in the Middle East begin in central Turkey. The Euphrates River (called the Firat in Turkey) has its headwaters near Elazig and flows southeast first into Syria and then into Iraq. The Tigris River (the Dicle in Turkey) has its source close to the Euphrates and flows south past both the important oil-producing area of Mosul in Iraq and the Iraqi capital of Baghdad.

The Tigris and Euphrates rivers helped to form the Fertile Crescent, a delta with rich soil and plenty of water, where some of the earliest civilizations in the Middle East began. In Turkey, however, these rivers pass through steep mountain gorges, providing the country mainly with hydroelectric power.

A ship enters the Bosporus and steams toward the spires of Istanbul.

Also of importance are several smaller rivers that water various areas of the country. The Menderes and Gediz rivers begin in western Turkey and flow to the Aegean Sea, while the Yesil Irmak and Kizil Irmak rivers start in eastern areas of the country and empty into the Black Sea. The Seyhan River irrigates the cotton fields of Adana before running into the Mediterranean Sea.

Climate

Turkey's climate is greatly influenced by its topography. The area along the coasts of Anatolia—in the narrow, lowland strips at the foot of the mountains—is characterized by hot summers and cool winters. The southern Anatolian coast has a very warm climate and is known as the "Turkish Riviera." It is a region of palm trees and of mild seas that are ideal for swimming.

Inland, the climate changes greatly. Rainfall, which averages 20 to 30 inches annually along the coast, is greater in the mountains. It then tapers off in the dry grasslands of the Central Plateau. The city of Karaman, for example, receives only 14 inches of rain annually, and summer temperatures average about 70° F. Winter temperatures in the central region hover around the freezing point.

Winters in the east are very dry, except in the mountainous regions, which are blanketed by heavy snows and are characterized by bitterly cold temperatures. Kars, for example, a city near the Soviet border, has recorded temperatures of −40° F.

Flora and Fauna

The western and southern coasts of Turkey feature Mediterranean plant life, with

Courtesy of Cultural and Tourism Office of the Turkish Embassy

Although the history of Alanya stretches back to Roman times, the modern city—part of the Turkish Riviera—is known for its excellent beaches surrounded by rocky hillsides.

Lush forests cover the alpine areas of eastern Turkey.

Courtesy of Sarah Larson

Courtesy of Steve Feinstein

A field of sunflowers, which will be harvested and made into oil, thrives in the fertile land between Bursa and Izmir.

groves of pine, oak, chestnut, juniper, olive, and citrus trees. The coast of the Black Sea supports laurel and myrtle plants, as well as strawberry trees (European evergreens). The mountain areas along the Black Sea have more densely forested land, where stands of oak, elm, and beech trees are found. The Central Plateau of Anatolia is a semi-arid zone of grassy pastures and scattered forests. Few trees grow in the area, but low-level vegetation, such as vetches, spurges, and bulbs, are among the many short plants that thrive.

Since Anatolia has been a very heavily populated area for more than 3,000 years, the numbers of wild animals and their habitats have decreased with the advance of human settlement. Nevertheless, deer,

13

bears, wolves, wild boars, and many kinds of birds still live in the region. Because a bird migration route between the Middle East and northern Europe crosses Turkey, a rich diversity of bird life exists in the country.

Cities

Turkey has had four capitals since the fourteenth century. The first Ottoman capital was Bursa, located in the hills south of Istanbul in Asia Minor. Early European conquests led to the selection of Adrianople (named after the Roman emperor Hadrian and now called Edirne) as the second capital in the late fourteenth century. After conquering the third capital—Constantinople—in 1453, the Turks renamed it Istanbul, which remained the Turkish seat of power until the end of World War I. When national disintegration became a threat in the 1920s, Mustafa Kemal Ataturk—the founder of modern

A Roman-era aqueduct bridge, which once carried water over a river or small gulley, blends into the surroundings of modern Istanbul.

Bursa—Turkey's first Ottoman capital city—lies among the hillsides of northwestern Anatolia.

Ferries and small fishing boats dock at the sides of the Galata Bridge, which spans the Golden Horn, while cars and pedestrians cross overhead.

The Turkish government has made a great effort to eliminate Istanbul's slums, where unsanitary conditions affect the health standards of the residents.

Turkey—moved the Turkish capital to Ankara. Ataturk felt that Ankara, located in the central highlands, was closer to most of Turkey's population than Istanbul was.

Despite Ankara's recent promotion, Istanbul (population 2.8 million) is still the largest and most developed city in the country. Istanbul is separated by water at two places, dividing the city into three parts.

Uskudar, the eastern section of Istanbul located on the Asiatic side of the Straits, is characterized by its pink roofs, white-walled buildings, old graveyards, and new factories. The more populous, European side of Istanbul consists of two areas separated by the Golden Horn, a five-mile inlet that juts from the mouth of the Bosporus. Beyoglu, the northern section, has traditionally been home to the city's low-income groups, who live in crowded alleyways and, lately, in more

Among the stunning treasures of Istanbul is Topkapi Palace, which was built for Sultan Mehmed II in the fifteenth century.

In Ankara—Turkey's capital city since the founding of the republic—Guven Park is a pleasant place to escape the hustle and bustle of downtown traffic.

The Greek amphitheater at Ephesus was originally constructed in the third century B.C. After it was enlarged and rebuilt, the site could hold a crowd of 24,000 spectators.

Originally founded by Ionian Greeks in about 1000 B.C., Ephesus grew into a prosperous trading city. Its main street, called the Arcadiane, ran down to the ancient harbor.

modern suburbs. The skyline of the southern half of historic Istanbul reveals the sharp spires of religious buildings. Topkapi Palace, the Blue Mosque, the Suleymaniye Mosque, and Hagia Sophia are stunning architectural tributes to centuries of history.

Ankara, the Turkish capital since 1923, has a population of 2.5 million. Established in the eighth century on the site of a Hittite town, Ankara was taken by the Ottomans in 1356. Almost seven centuries later, the city became the focus of the nationalists during the Turkish war for independence. Like Istanbul, Ankara has buildings from many eras of Turkey's history standing alongside modern, Western structures that reveal the capital's twentieth-century direction.

Izmir, formerly called Smyrna, has 636,000 inhabitants and lies on the Aegean Sea. Famous as a resort city, Izmir is at the center of a region rich in Greco-Roman history. The ruins of Pergamum and Ephesus draw archaeologists and visitors from around the world. The area also is renowned for its delicious figs and seedless grapes.

Archaeologists discovered the site of Hattushash, the ancient Hittite capital, only a century ago. Huge doorways — such as the Lion Gate adorned with ceremonial figures — are found throughout the city's remains.

2) History and Government

Humans inhabited Turkey so long ago that no historical records of these early peoples exist. Archaeologists, however, have investigated ancient sites in Anatolia and have found evidence of prehistoric settlements. Among the most exciting finds are those of a Stone Age community at Catalhoyuk, near modern Konya.

Hittites and Assyrians

Turkey's first recorded history began about 4,000 years ago. At that time, the Hittites, a warrior group that originated in the Caucasus Mountains of eastern Europe, lived in Anatolia. Knowledge of these peoples comes from clay-tablet writings kept by foreign merchants living in Anatolia who traded with the Hittites. By about 1750 B.C. the Hittites had united into a single, powerful kingdom, which began absorbing realms to the south.

Under a succession of able kings, the Hittites expanded in all directions, bringing many different peoples and cultures — including the Egyptians and Syrians — into their empire. The empire prospered until about the twelfth century B.C. when, according to Egyptian sources, a seafaring people conquered the region. Thereafter, the kingdom survived only in the form of small city-states, such as Carchemish.

The Assyrian Empire, located southeast of the Hittite city-states, eventually absorbed the weakened kingdom in about 715 B.C. Almost entirely dependent on its army for stability, the Assyrian Empire collapsed only a century after taking over the Hittite territories. After that, regional political units—such as the Phrygian and Lydian kingdoms—developed in Turkey.

Greeks and Persians

In the eighth century B.C., Greeks—Dorians, Ionians, and Aeolians—began to cross the Aegean Sea and to settle along present-day Turkey's western shores. Cities such as Ephesus, Halicarnassus, Miletus, and Troy prospered as trading centers through Greek influence.

By the sixth century B.C., the Lydians had conquered most of the Greek cities and had amassed great wealth. Croesus, the last king of Lydia, extended his empire over much of Anatolia and constantly sought to increase his wealth and power by conquest. He fought against the Persian Empire located to the east but was defeated in battle in 546 B.C.

Large stone carvings of King Antiochus Epiphanes IV and Zeus were part of a holy place built 2,000 years ago near Adiyaman in southern Turkey.

The Persians sacked the Temple of Apollo at Didyma in 494 B.C. Rebuilding began two centuries later but was never completed.

A silver tetradrachm coin—issued in 323 B.C., the year Alexander the Great died—shows the head of Hercules *(top)* on the front. The back *(bottom)* depicts Zeus (the strongest of the Greek gods) enthroned, holding a royal scepter and an eagle. The Greek lettering translates as "Alexander the king."

The Greek cities of Asia Minor remained under the control of their new Persian overlords for several centuries. With the help of Greeks from Athens, the Greeks of Asia revolted against the Persians in 499 B.C. Although they made repeated attempts to defeat the Greeks, the Persians were beaten in battle after battle.

As the power of the Persian Empire waned, a young warrior from Macedon—an area in northwestern Greece that included Thrace—inherited his father's throne. Alexander III (called the Great), the new king of Macedon, used his brilliant military strategies to swing the balance of power in his direction. On one of his campaigns, he crossed the Dardanelles to destroy the Persian Empire in Asia Minor.

At the time of his death in 323 B.C., Alexander the Great ruled over the largest empire—including all of present-day Turkey—that the ancient world had ever known.

The Roman and Byzantine Empires

After Alexander's death, his empire crumbled into many small factions. The resulting political and economic turmoil lasted for more than two centuries until the area, including much of modern Turkey, was added to the Roman Empire. Roman rule brought peace and prosperity to Asia Minor for several hundred years. The eastern part of the empire became so economically important that in A.D. 326 the Roman emperor Constantine I moved his capital to the old Greek city of Byzantium on the shores of the Bosporus. On this site he built a modern capital called New Rome, soon renamed Constantinople (Constantine's City).

Christian artworks—such as this fresco (a painting on plaster) of Jesus—are found in isolated holy places throughout Turkey.

With Constantine's conversion to Christianity, Constantinople became the seat of the Christianized Roman Empire. In A.D. 395, as part of an empirewide reorganization, the Latin-speaking western section of the empire was separated from the Greek-speaking eastern part. Thereafter, Constantinople was the center of the eastern realm, later called the Byzantine Empire.

For more than a thousand years the Byzantine Empire and Constantinople survived, despite invasions and internal corruption. In the seventh century, the empire included all of Anatolia and Greece, as well as Syria, Egypt, the island of Sicily in the Mediterranean Sea, most of Italy, and parts of North Africa and the Balkans (now Eastern Europe). As the richest area of the empire, Anatolia provided the largest portion of the fighting force that protected the far-reaching imperial borders.

Constantinople—the nerve center of this sprawling power—was repeatedly attacked. The first great threat to the Byzantine Empire came from Arab armies, who were inspired to fight by the new religion of Islam. Although slowly diminishing in size, the empire also survived attacks by Slavic, Persian, and Germanic invaders until the eleventh century A.D.

At that time, armies from Western Europe organized into religious crusades. These forces passed through Constantinople on their way to the Holy Land in the Middle East, which they hoped to free from Islamic domination. The members of the fourth crusade, however, turned on the Byzantine Empire, capturing and looting Constantinople in 1204. The crusaders established a Western-style state, called the Latin Empire. The Byzantine government did not regain control of Constantinople until 1261.

Courtesy of Sarah Larson

From the seventh to eleventh centuries, Muslim armies attacked and burned Christian buildings, such as this chapel, in an effort to spread the religion of Islam.

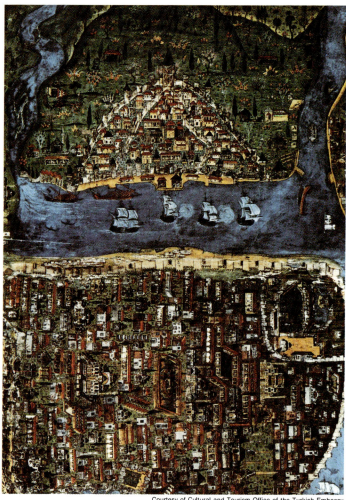

Miniatures are small, handcrafted pictures, usually of historical importance. Istanbul *(left)* is depicted surrounded by its sturdy walls overlooking the Golden Horn to Galata. Another work *(opposite)* shows Sultan Suleyman I fully dressed for battle. Suleyman, who ruled from 1520 to 1566, was called "the Magnificent" by Westerners and "the Lawgiver" by the Turks. During his reign, much of Eastern Europe was added to the Ottoman Empire.

Courtesy of Cultural and Tourism Office of the Turkish Embassy

Turks Arrive from Turkistan

During the tenth century Turkish farmers began moving into Anatolia. These peoples from the arid steppes of central Asia were forced out of their homeland, called Turkistan, by the Mongols, a stronger and better-organized Asian group. Newcomers to the country that now bears their name, the Turks settled down among the mixture of peoples in Anatolia. From contact with the Arabs, the Turks adopted the Islamic religion. One group of Turks, the Seljuks, seized political control of almost all of Anatolia from the faltering Byzantine Empire and established a kingdom called the Sultanate of Rum in the twelfth century.

During the thirteenth century, in a small district of northwestern Anatolia, a Turk named Ertugrul became the local ruler and founder of the dynasty of Ottoman Turks. In the centuries that followed, Ertugrul's descendants expanded their rule to include most of the Middle East and large parts of Europe and North Africa. The name Ottoman is derived from Osman, the name of Ertugrul's son and successor.

Ottoman Rule Is Established

The Ottoman Turks expanded their dominions rapidly at the expense of the Byzantine Greeks and the collapsing Seljuks.

Courtesy of Cultural and Tourism Office of the Turkish Embassy

A military parade shows the excellent training that made Ottoman troops hard to defeat in battle.

Under Sultan (the Turkish name for a king or emperor) Orhan I, the Ottomans crossed the Dardanelles in 1345 and gained their first foothold in Europe at Gallipoli, from which they proceeded to invade much of the Western world. The Ottoman Empire progressed with the help of Christian kings in the Balkans who invited the Ottomans to settle conflicts with other local rulers. To the surprise of these Balkan monarchs, however, the Turks had no plans for leaving the battlefield once the fighting was over.

As evidence of their success in Europe, the Turks moved their capital in 1366 from Bursa in Anatolia to Adrianople in eastern Europe. Kingdoms in Serbia, Romania, and Bulgaria fell to the Turks, but they

Known in Turkish as *Aya Sofya,* Hagia Sophia (Divine Wisdom) is the third Christian church so named to be located on this site. Previous churches were destroyed by fire during political riots. After one such riot in the sixth century, the Roman emperor Justinian had the church rebuilt and opened the structure in A.D. 537. Although the building has been restored at various times, it looks much as it did in Justinian's time.

The sultan had absolute civil and religious power within the Ottoman Empire and held meetings with his advisers at will.

itary conquest and on religious conversion to Islam. Called ghazis (warriors of the faith), these early Turks were a closely knit society that invaded the Middle East, Anatolia, and southeastern Europe from central Asia.

By the mid-fifteenth century, the Turks had taken over the lands and the cultures of great civilizations, which had collapsed as the Turkish armies invaded. Indeed, it was said that the two main functions of the Ottoman government were to make war and to collect taxes to finance warmaking activities. Except within the family structure, even upper-class Ottoman women had little power or visibility.

Islam provided the Ottoman Turks with a written language—Arabic—as well as with the essentials of the Islamic religion and culture. The sultan became both leader of the civil government and caliph (head of the Islamic religion).

failed to capture Constantinople for nearly 100 years.

In 1453 the Turks stormed the city's battlements and seized the capital, renaming it Istanbul, from the Greek phrase *eis tan polin,* meaning "to the city." Sultan Mohammed II immediately ordered the famous Byzantine church of Hagia Sophia to be converted into a mosque (an Islamic holy place). This change symbolized the transformation of Christian Constantinople into the capital of a great Islamic empire. According to a census taken 25 years later, 60 percent of all households in Istanbul were Muslim, that is, they followed the Islamic religion.

The Shaping of the Empire

Males in the Ottoman Empire followed a warrior philosophy that focused on mil-

A male-dominated world, the Ottoman Empire gave women—even those of noble birth—little freedom.

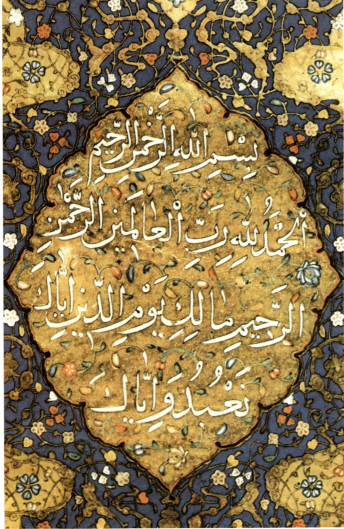

A verse from an illuminated Koran (book of sacred Islamic writings) dates from the sixteenth century. The teachings of the Koran—and their interpretation by Islamic religious leaders—could influence the sultan's decisions.

Courtesy of Cultural and Tourism Office of the Turkish Embassy

The center of Ottoman power after 1453 was Topkapi Palace in Istanbul, where the sultan and his entire court lived. The sultan presided over a council of advisers called the divan, as well as over a number of schools for educating young people for jobs in the imperial bureaucracy. For those who held government positions, advancement was possible. A few individuals attained high office—some reaching the post of grand vizier, the most powerful adviser in the divan.

Powerful Influences

As part of the rewards of conquest, the Ottomans acquired many slaves. Some of these people were the children of Christians from the Balkan provinces of southeastern Europe. Taken to the royal court in Istanbul, male slaves were converted to Islam, educated, and organized into a strong fighting legion called the Janissary Corps (taken from *yeniçeri*, the Turkish word for "new troops"). The corps served both as an imperial body guard and as a unit of the Turkish army. Because of their superb training, the Janissaries would be sent into battle at critical moments to give the Ottomans a surprise advantage.

In the mid-sixteenth century, only 12,000 Janissaries served the empire, but by 1826 the corps numbered more than 135,000. As the Turkish state became involved in fewer wars, the restless Janissaries began to turn their energies to politics. Eventually, the corps became a disruptive force that could support or depose the sultan at will. When the power of the sultans started to decline in the seventeenth century, the Janissaries took it upon themselves to remove officials they did not like and shaped state policy to their own advantage.

Another powerful aspect of sultanic leadership was the ruler's harem, where his most important wives, children, and concubines, or secondary wives, lived. (Polygamy, or having more than one spouse at a time, was an accepted part of the Islamic religion.) At times, wives joined forces with military officers to gain influence, for it was believed that whoever could control the sultan could run the state. Occasionally, skilled but ruthless administrators, such as the Koprulu family of the seventeenth century, tried to bring order to the poorly run Ottoman royal house.

In addition to the power of the Janissary Corps and the residents of the seraglio (palace), religious leaders also had strong influence over the affairs of the empire. For example, the entire legal system of the Ottoman Empire was directed by Muslim religious scholars and judges. All laws

Surrounded by his advisers, Sultan Suleyman I receives the son of the king of Hungary at the Ottoman court.

Courtesy of Cultural and Tourism Office of the Turkish Embassy

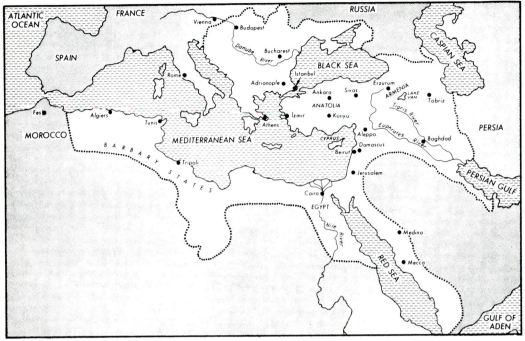

By the middle of the seventeenth century, the Ottoman Empire included all of the Middle East, much of the North African coast, and most of Eastern Europe. Map taken from *The Area Handbook for the Republic of Turkey*, 1973.

were in accord with the sacred writings, called the Koran, that form the basis of Islamic teaching.

As the Ottoman state tried to move toward reform in the seventeenth and eighteenth centuries, the Islamic establishment became resistant to change. Furthermore, the Janissaries—powerful beyond all control—also opposed new ideas and innovations that would weaken their position. As its European neighbors began to advance in areas of commerce and technology, the Ottoman Empire was hampered by its long-held traditions and values.

The Fall of the Janissaries

In 1826 Sultan Mahmud II decided to try to achieve two goals: the elimination of the Janissaries, because they threatened the stability of the state, and the introduction of Western-style modernization. In order to provoke the Janissaries, Mahmud commanded them to dress and march in Western style. When they rebelled and tried to storm the palace, they were killed by troops loyal to the sultan. About 25,000 Janissaries died during three days of fighting in Istanbul.

The violent end of the corps marked the beginning of a reform period in the Ottoman Empire, generally referred to as the *Tanzimat* (Turkish for reorganization), during which Western ideas, laws, and technology were gradually brought into the Ottoman world. Although the Janissaries never regained their powerful place in Ottoman affairs, occasional governmental improvements were not enough to halt the decline of the empire.

The Empire Weakens

During the eighteenth and nineteenth centuries, the center of power had shifted from the Ottoman Empire to Russia, Great Britain, France, Austria, and other European nations. Aware of the empire's weakened position, Europeans began to refer to it as "the sick man of Europe" and to help themselves to bits of Ottoman land.

Attempts to divide up the Ottoman Empire among European nations became known as the Eastern Question. The division would have happened much faster if the Europeans had not argued among themselves over which country was to get what part of the sultan's lands. Eventually, the French gained extensive Ottoman territories in 1740. The Russians demanded control of present-day Romania and the Straits for access to the Mediterranean Sea and the Middle East. In addition, sections within the Ottoman Empire rebelled. Greece, for example, won its independence in a war between 1820 and 1829.

Wars with Russia

During the nineteenth century, Great Britain decided to preserve the Ottoman Empire as a barrier to Russian expansion. Britain and France even joined the Ottomans against the Russians during the Crimean War from 1854 to 1856. The defeat of the Russians in Crimea, a peninsula in the Black Sea, temporarily restrained their ambitions to acquire Turkish lands. About 20 years later, however, the Turks engaged in another eastern European war against Russia.

After this second conflict was over, the Congress of Berlin created the independent states of Romania, Bulgaria, Albania, Serbia, and Montenegro, all of which were former territories of the Ottoman Empire. Moreover, the island of Cyprus came under British protection, and other Ottoman provinces were given to Austria. Later, the North African possessions were divided among Britain, France, and Italy.

The Young Turks

The decline of the Ottoman Empire provoked a revolution in Istanbul in 1908, led by a group known as the Young Turks.

Initially, their aim was to achieve a strong, unified nation by imposing a more centralized government directed by a legislature. The fears of traditionalists within the Ottoman Empire and the interference of foreign powers limited the impact of the reforms of the Young Turks. Eventually, the new government became a three-person military dictatorship, which focused on economic and military modernization. The administration of the Young Turks lasted through the twentieth century's first global conflict.

World War I

When the First World War broke out in 1914, the Ottoman Empire joined the

Courtesy of Cultural and Tourism Office of the Turkish Embassy

A thoughtful Mustafa Kemal climbs among the rocks at Gallipoli, the peninsula he and his Turkish troops successfully defended in World War I.

Central Powers—Germany, Austria-Hungary, and Bulgaria. Turkish hatred of the Russians (who with Britain and France were called the Allies), combined with economic aid from Germany, made it fairly easy for Turkey to side with the Central Powers.

Among the many poorly executed battles of World War I was the Gallipoli campaign, an Allied plan to knock the Ottoman Empire out of the war by seizing the Straits and choking Turkey's lines of supply. The attack, however, was a disaster, due both to Allied blunders and to a vigorous Turkish defense led by a young commander named Mustafa Kemal.

Although the Turks were able to defend their possessions in Anatolia, all of their Middle Eastern holdings were lost during the Arab-British military campaigns of 1917 and 1918. The British attacked from the Suez Canal region into Palestine (nearly coextensive with present-day Israel) and from Iran into Mesopotamia (modern Iraq). The Arabs captured the lands from the east bank of the Jordan River to Damascus. Faced with a worsening military situation, the Turks signed a peace agreement on October 30, 1918.

The Turks had lost 325,000 soldiers in battle but counted more than 2 million civilian casualties. This high proportion of deaths included about 1.5 million Armenians, a Christian ethnic group of eastern Turkey. Fearing that the Armenians would help Christian Russia during the war, the Turks massacred them in enormous numbers.

The Treaty of Sèvres and Its Aftermath

After the war, Allied leaders sliced up Turkey's territory into small pieces under the Treaty of Sèvres. Under the agreement, France would control Lebanon and Syria, and Britain was to be awarded Iraq, Transjordan (present-day Jordan), and Palestine. Greece was to take parts of Thrace and the lands surrounding Smyrna (modern Izmir). Italy would get the Antalya region of southwestern Anatolia, and

Courtesy of Cultural and Tourism Office of the Turkish Embassy

A Turkish painting depicts the recovery of a village during the civil conflict in Turkey that followed the First World War.

Mustafa Kemal stands outside the newly established Grand National Assembly in Ankara in 1920. Kemal served as the assembly's first president.

the people of Kurdistan, in northeastern Turkey, were to decide their own future in a regional vote. The Straits, as well as the finances of Turkey, were to be under European control.

Many Turks, including Mustafa Kemal, refused to accept the settlement described in the Treaty of Sèvres. A nationalist movement—which eventually grew into a full-scale civil war—developed under Kemal's leadership. A temporary revolutionary government was set up in Ankara (the nationalists' headquarters), and the new regime proclaimed self-rule in 1921.

Backed by a strong military force and a working political organization, Kemal attracted negotiation efforts from several of the Allied powers. The Soviet Union—which resulted from the Russian Revolution of 1917—absorbed what remained of the Armenian territories in exchange for a quiet border with Turkey. Thousands of Greeks, Armenians, and Turks died in battles near Smyrna, and the British—the

European power patrolling the territory—avoided an additional clash by allowing the Turks to control Thrace.

The Turks renegotiated the Treaty of Sèvres in 1922. The agreements resulting from the Conference of Lausanne gave back to Turkey all of Anatolia, except the Straits, which remained under Allied control until 1938. The Turks, in turn, agreed to surrender the Arab parts of the Ottoman Empire.

Birth of the Republic

Seven hundred years of Ottoman rule came to an end when Mustafa Kemal declared the foundation of the Republic of Turkey on October 29, 1923. Although Turkey had a new constitution and was supposed to be a democracy, the real power of the government remained in the hands of Kemal and his assistants. Kemal, who changed his name to Ataturk ("Father of the Turks") in 1928, was a dictator. His highly authoritarian actions were aimed at transforming the nation from a traditional society into a modern, Western-style state —a change that Kemal believed would benefit the Turkish people.

A series of new laws completely altered Turkish society. The government broke the control of Muslim religious leaders, who opposed change in Turkish life. This action separated religion and the state and closed down Muslim courts and religious schools. A law code patterned after Switzerland's legal tradition replaced the old Islamic law. Women no longer wore veils in public, and they received the right to vote. The new regime also began many other reforms based on practices in the West, including the use of family names and the introduction of the Western alphabet, Western numerals, and a more modern calendar.

By the time of Ataturk's death in 1938, Turkey had regained its place among the independent nations of the world. Much remained to be done, but a solid base for future progress had been laid down by Ataturk and his associates. Turkey's return as a world power was recognized when the Allies returned control of the Straits in 1938.

During World War II from 1939 to 1945, Turkey was determined to remain neutral. This decision placed the country in a difficult position, because, before the war,

Independent Picture Service

An aging Ataturk—the name taken by Kemal when he began the use of Turkish last names—speaks intently to a group of Turkish schoolchildren.

Ataturk's successor as president and leader of the Republican People's party was Ismet Inonu *(left)*, shown in conversation with diplomat Averell Harriman of the United States.

most of its trade had been with Germany. Finally, Turkey declared war on Germany on February 23, 1945, mainly to gain acceptance as a charter member of the United Nations.

The Era After World War II

At the end of World War II, Ismet Inonu, Ataturk's successor, and his Republican People's party decided that Turkey was ready to begin genuine democratic rule. Political opposition developed under the Democrat party, and in the elections of 1950 the Democrats won by a wide margin. For 10 years, under the leadership of Adnan Menderes, the Democrat party remained in power. But by the mid-1950s, economic difficulties began to arise. When political demonstrations erupted, the Democrats tried to restrain freedom of speech and of the press, as well as to discredit opposition candidates.

After some violent student protests, members of the Turkish army seized control of the government on May 27, 1960, and jailed the Democrat party leaders. Within a year, General Cemal Gursel, leader of the military coup, ended the temporary military regime and held elections in accordance with the constitution. In May 1961 he resigned from the army and was elected president.

Turkey and Cyprus

The longest-lasting international problem for Turkey since the end of World War II has involved Cyprus, an island off Turkey's southern border. Cyprus's population—consisting of 80 percent Greeks and 20 percent Turks—has had a long history of internal conflict. The Turks feared that Greece would use the majority rule principle to justify claiming Cyprus as part of Greek territory, a move that would cause great difficulties for the Turks who lived on the island.

In 1960 the issue was partially resolved by creating the Republic of Cyprus, whose independence was guaranteed jointly by Great Britain, Greece, and Turkey. In the years that followed, however, Greeks on the island tried to impose enosis, or unification, with Greece. In 1974, after Greece supported a secret buildup of military power on Cyprus, Turkey invaded and occupied one-third of the island. In 1983, after nine years of occupation, the Turkish Cypriots declared a Turkish Republic of Northern Cyprus. Turkey, however, is the only country to recognize Northern Cyprus as a nation.

The Modern Era

The Turkish military has continued to play a visible role in Turkish politics. In March 1971, after the ruling Justice party failed to control civilian violence, the army took control of the situation. The period between 1971 and 1980 produced frequent shifts of power between the Justice party, led by Suleyman Demirel, and the Republican People's party, headed by Bulent Ecevit. Neither party was able to win the confidence of the people, and violence increased. The army again seized the reins of government in 1980, under the leadership of General Kenan Evren. Elections were held in 1983, and the winner was the Motherland party. Its leader, Turgut Ozal, became prime minister, and General Evren took on the more powerful job of president.

Turkey's government made strides toward returning the nation to democratic practices in the late 1980s. In July 1987 the Turkish government lifted martial law (military rule) in the last four provinces that had been under military authority. A special public vote in September 1987 cancelled a measure that had banned some opposition figures from politics. Elections in November of that year completed Turkey's return to civilian rule.

Unrest in eastern Turkey increased during the 1980s, fueled in part by the government's treatment of the Kurds, most of whom live in the area. Human rights organizations, such as Amnesty International, suggest that torture of political prisoners —of whom there were nearly 180,000 in Turkey in the late 1980s—is widespread. The accusation, which the government denies, has further tarnished its image.

The Government

The Constitution of 1982 states that Turkey is a republic. Members of the legislative branch, which is called the Grand National Assembly, are elected for five-year terms. The assembly appoints the president, who has a nonrenewable term of seven years. The powers of the president were vastly expanded after 1983. The president can veto constitutional amendments, submit referendums, dissolve the legislature, and call for new elections.

The president also selects judges for the military and civilian courts. The prime minister, who is appointed by the president, is responsible for the daily administration of the government. Turkey has 67 provinces, which are divided into districts and townships. Each province is headed by a vali, who represents the government, and each province has its own elective council.

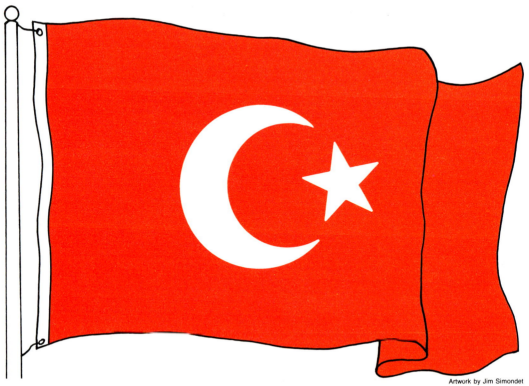

Artwork by Jim Simondet

In coloring its flag, the Turkish republic followed the design used during the Ottoman Empire. The crescent moon and the star once were symbols in both the Roman and Christian religions, but they became associated with Islam—and particularly with Ottoman rule—in the fifteenth century.

A Kurdish mother and son—members of Turkey's largest, non-Turkish minority—live in Siverek, a town in the southeastern part of the country.

Photo by Robert Fried

3) The People

The Turkish population is growing rapidly—at an annual rate of 2.2 percent—which means that the number of Turks will double within 32 years. According to the 1960 census, the population was 27.8 million. In 1988 the population estimate exceeded 52.9 million. About 55 percent of the people live in rural areas and are dependent on subsistence farming, that is, they raise only enough food to feed their families.

Although the people of Turkey are called Turks, they are a mixture of many ethnic groups. Every conquering nation that settled in Turkey has affected the makeup of the population. Hittite, Greek, and Persian empires have made the major contributions to Turkish backgrounds, although the arrival of the central Asian Seljuks also introduced ethnic traits. The Kurds, living in the southeastern part of the country and numbering about four million, are the largest, distinctly non-Turkish minority. Their ancestors were Aryans, an Asian people who moved to the area by at least the tenth century. Many Kurds have light hair and blue eyes, in contrast to the dark hair and brown eyes of the Turks. In addition—despite the massacres of the early twentieth century—Turkey still has a large Armenian population.

The Arts

Turkey—one of the centers of world architecture—has a great mosque-building tradition, which stems from the Islamic religion. After the Ottoman takeover in 1453, Turkish builders reached new heights of architectural excellence and produced notable landmarks.

Turkish architectural designs came partially from the Seljuks, whose style evolved slowly as they absorbed Arab culture. In addition, when the Turks conquered the city of Constantinople, they inherited a rich legacy from the Byzantine Empire. They readily adopted the style of the basilica of Hagia Sophia, which had been constructed by the Christian emperor

Courtesy of Sarah Larson

These two men are from a rural area of western Turkey. About 55 percent of the national population lives in the countryside.

Independent Picture Service

Topkapi Palace—where the sultan and his entire court lived in Ottoman times—is now a museum and contains some of Turkey's most treasured artworks. In addition, the palace itself, first built in the late fifteenth century on an ancient, fortified site, is a splendid example of rambling, imperial architecture. The buildings and courtyards cover an area that is larger than Vatican City and about half the size of the principality of Monaco.

Standing side by side in Istanbul are hallmarks of the city's long history. Hagia Sophia *(background far left)* is a Byzantine masterpiece of the sixth century A.D. The closest obelisk, or pillar, shows the damage done by crusading armies in 1204. The Blue Mosque *(far right)* — the only one with six turrets — was constructed by the Ottomans in the seventeenth century.

Justinian in the sixth century A.D. The Turks studied and analyzed this place of worship, converted it into a mosque for their own use, and made it the model for most mosques built around Istanbul and other large cities of the Ottoman world.

The ornate doorway of Ince Minare Medresesi — a religious institution opened in 1258 in the Seljuk capital of Konya — shows the skill of Seljuk stone carvers.

The architectural splendor of Hagia Sophia *(above)* inspired the Ottoman Turks to build their mosques in a similar style.

In a land where few people could read or write until the twentieth century, miniatures served to record important events in Ottoman history. Here, the Ottoman forces are depicted attacking Halq al-Wadi—the port of the city of Tunis, Tunisia—in 1575.

Courtesy of Cultural and Tourism Office of the Turkish Embassy

Turkish art before the nineteenth century focused mainly on the production of miniatures—highly colored works painted on small canvasses with exacting detail—which was a tradition imported from Persia. This intricate art form has become an important feature of Turkish art history, as well as a form of period documentation of the Ottoman Empire. In the twentieth century, Turkey has gradually developed a nonreligious artistic style, which has appeared more often since the 1930s, when separation from Islam was a national priority.

A rich craft tradition still exists, which is displayed in the bazaars, or street markets, of Turkey's cities. The artisanship of hammered brass and copper, ceramics, jewelry design and manufacture, furniture making, and rug weaving is still strong in Turkey.

Language and Literature

Originally adopted by the Seljuks, the Turkish language is spoken by nearly everyone in Turkey. Turkish is an imported tongue of the Ural-Altaic language group, which has its center between the Ural and Altai mountains of the Soviet Union. Yet Turkey once was home to peoples who spoke Indo-European lan-

At a streetside market, a rug maker—surrounded by colorful examples of his skill—bends over another carpet.

guages, which include Greek and Persian. In isolated areas, such as Kurdistan, local residents still speak their native tongues.

Turkish literature represents a mixture of styles taken from the many peoples the Turks have encountered throughout their history. Before the arrival of Islam, Persian literature probably had the greatest impact, but when Islam appeared, Persian and Muslim traditions continued side by side. Turks were especially fond of poetry, and the ghazel, a short poem that praised love and wine, was the main form. In addition, mystical traditions from the East further enriched Turkish poetry and literature.

In the nineteenth century a new form of writing, called Tanzimat literature, developed. A result of the contact between the Ottoman Empire and the West, this tradition introduced new writing structures, such as novels, short stories, plays, and Western-style essays. Later in the century, nationalist literature—inspired by the

Sultan Mahmud II wrote this four-line Turkish prayer in *Taliq*—an ornate Arabic script.

writings of Ziya Gokalp—emphasized Turkishness and focused on stories about rural life, urban problems, and social themes.

Modern writers, such as Fakir Baykurt, Mahmut Makal, and Yashar Kemal, lead the way in a Turkish literary revival. Kemal's work, *Mehmet, My Hawk*, is among the nation's most popular works and has been translated into more than a dozen languages. Makal's *Our Village* exposed the hardships of rural life in Anatolia. Poetry still continues to be important, and Fazi Hunsnu Daglarca is among the most famous poets. Simple storytelling—such as the exploits of Karagoz (Black Eyes), a shadow puppet who has many adventures and who outwits his enemies—is favored in towns and villages.

Religion

About 98 percent of Turkey's population are Muslim, but other religions are guaranteed the right to exist in Turkey without

Facing toward Mecca—the birthplace of Muhammad, the founder of the Islamic religion—a lone Muslim says his daily prayers.

The plight of Turkey's rural populations, many of whom once lived in dismal conditions, inspired Mahmut Makal to write *Our Village*.

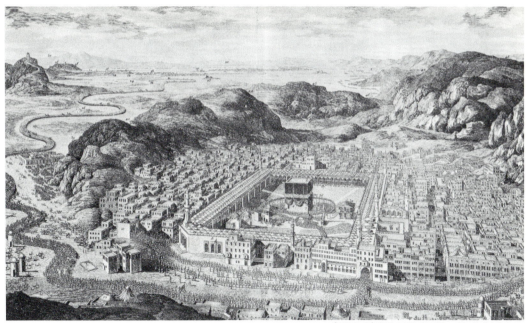

Courtesy of Cultural and Tourism Office of the Turkish Embassy

An engraving shows Al-Haram, the most sacred mosque in Mecca, and thousands of pilgrims making the hajj. The black block in the courtyard of the mosque is the Kaaba, believed to have been built by the prophet Abraham, from whom both Muslims and Jews claim descent.

Independent Picture Service

Although females are no longer required to wear veils, many village women still cover their heads.

interference. Muslim Turks are mostly members of the Sunni sect—the orthodox, or most traditional, branch of Islam.

Faithful Muslims are expected to pray five times every day while facing in the direction of Mecca, the birthplace of Muhammad, the great Islamic prophet. The piercing call of a muezzin—the Muslim crier who stands high up in the minaret, or tower, of a mosque—summons Muslims to prayer. If it is possible, Muslims are to make a pilgrimage, called the hajj, to the holy city of Mecca at least once during their lives. Every year hundreds of thousands of Muslims from all parts of the world, including Turkey, make the hajj.

Although Turkey has many mosques in which the faithful may pray, the number of active worshippers is small compared to the total number of Muslims. This lessened interest can be traced partly to Ataturk's drive to Westernize Turkey. His discontinuation of some religious traditions—such as the women's veil and the

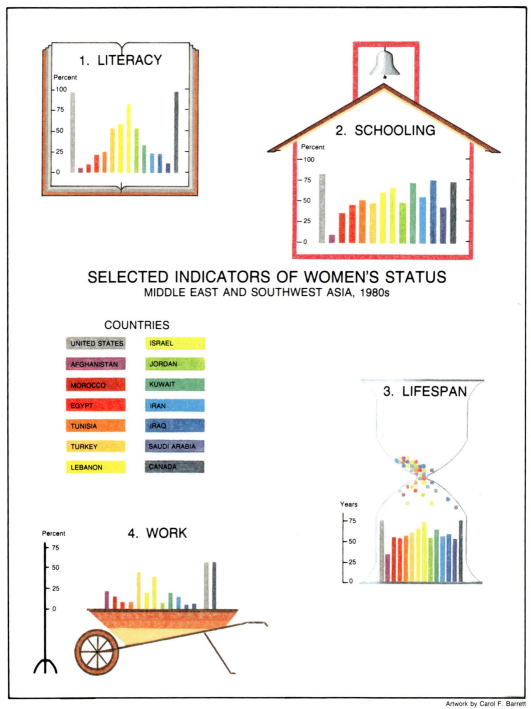

Depicted in this chart are factors relating to the status of women in the Middle East and southwest Asia. Graph 1, labeled Literacy, shows the percentage of adult women who can read and write. Graph 2 illustrates the proportion of school-aged girls who actually attend elementary and secondary schools. Graph 3 depicts the life expectancy of female babies at birth. Graph 4 shows the percentage of women in the income-producing work force. Data taken from *Women in the World: An International Atlas,* 1986 and from *Women . . . A World Survey,* 1985.

A bride and groom display the woman's dowry—the goods she brings to her marriage—at an Islamic wedding in Dogubeyazit, a town in eastern Turkey near the Iranian border.

connection of Muslim religious leaders with the judicial system—has caused considerable tension among Muslims. In some ways, therefore, Islam has become identified more with Turkey's past than with its present and future. Among those who live in the countryside, however, Islam still has a large, active following.

Education

During the time of the Ottoman Empire, little was done to develop a national system of education. Students from families wealthy enough to send their children to school spent long hours learning the difficult Arabic alphabet used in the Turkish language. Schools often stressed memori-

Children gather outside their school in Antalya, Turkey. The government has made great efforts to increase the literacy rate, which was 70 percent in the 1980s.

zation of passages from the Koran, the Muslim collection of holy writings, instead of courses directly related to the modern world. The founders of the Turkish republic realized that, if Turkey was to become an industrialized country, its schools would have to be drastically updated.

Ataturk and his followers moved swiftly. For the first time, educational planning was done on a nationwide basis. All connections between schools and the Muslim religion were broken, and only the government controlled education. One of Ataturk's most striking innovations was to replace the Arabic script with a modified form of the Latin alphabet, in which Western languages are written. This change represented the fact that modern Turkey had turned away from the Middle East and had opened new channels of communication with the West.

One of the great aims of the Turkish government is to wipe out illiteracy by providing free and compulsory primary education for all children. Bringing schooling to every part of the nation is a very ambitious undertaking. In the more remote areas that lack funds, teachers, and supplies, the mountainous terrain further hampers educational efforts. The rapid increase in population has also placed new demands on the educational system.

Turkish secondary education provides technical and vocational training, in addition to preparatory courses for those intending to continue to the university level. Turkish universities are located in Istanbul, Ankara, Izmir, and Erzurum. Graduates from universities, technical schools, and teacher-training colleges lead the constant struggle to further Turkey's industrialization.

Courtesy of CARE

By watching an older craftsman, these Turkish boys learn the art of wood carving.

Ankara's Middle East Technical University, whose library is used by both students and faculty, was set up in 1957 to meet Turkey's need for trained engineers, scientists, and technicians.

In the early 1980s, almost 40 percent of Turks over the age of six had had some primary education. The literacy rate—only 10 percent in 1927—was approaching 70 percent in the 1980s, although almost five million more males than females were literate. Roughly 6.5 million pupils were enrolled in primary schools, almost 2 million in secondary schools, and about 900,000 in institutions of higher learning. In 1979 there were 18 universities, and by 1982, 8 more campuses had been founded.

Health

The Turkish government pays for health care for the poor. Urban areas have the most doctors and the best medical facilities, and people in rural areas sometimes suffer from preventable diseases because of the shortage of professional care. Large-scale immunization campaigns that began in the mid-1980s have had some success in preventing diseases that affect children.

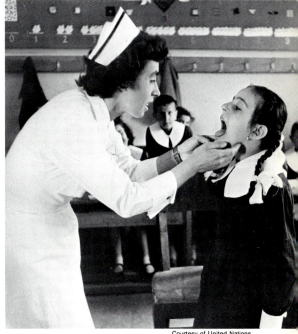
A visiting nurse checks a young student's mouth and throat at the Demielibahee Primary School in Ankara. Urban areas continue to have better health facilities than rural regions.

Baklava, a Turkish dessert that translates literally as lozenge, is a sticky-sweet concoction of nuts, honey, and thin pastry.

Courtesy of Turkish Consulate General

Other programs have begun to combat major infections—such as tuberculosis and trachoma (an eye disease)—but progress is slow. In 1987 only one physician existed for every 1,465 people, and there was one hospital bed available for every 475 patients who needed one. Life expectancy in 1988 was 63 years of age, while infant mortality stood at 95 deaths in every 1,000 live births, both of which are average figures for the region but which are worse than Western statistics. About 36 percent of the population are under 15 years of age, and 4 percent are over age 65.

Food

With its many ethnic and cultural influences, Turkey enjoys a wide range of foods. In the countryside, cracked wheat bread and creamy yogurt make up most of the local diet. Meat and rice are expensive for most Turks and, consequently, are eaten sparingly. On special occasions, however, Turks celebrate with dishes such as shish kebab—skewered chunks of lamb and vegetables cooked over a flame. A favorite dessert is baklava, which consists of paper-thin sheets of pastry layered with honey and chopped nuts. Coffee, served

A cook in Bursa prepares to make a doner kebab sandwich. He shaves off thin slices of meat from a large piece of lamb, which has been broiled on a turning shaft. The meat slices may be tucked inside pita, or pocket, bread along with onions, tomatoes, and other vegetables.

Courtesy of Steve Feinstein

Athletes compete in the Greased Wrestling Festival held each year in Edirne, near the Greek border.

A food vendor in Istanbul grills small chunks of spiced meats to tempt passersby.

thick and sweet, is a popular beverage, as is raki, an alcoholic mixture made from raisins.

Sports

Turks are great recreation enthusiasts, and soccer is probably their most important sport. With a horse population of several hundred thousand, Turkey also supports avid riding and racing fans. Another sport, greased wrestling, is also a popular event, especially at fairs and festivals. To make the wrestling holds more difficult, participants cover their bodies with olive oil.

Hunters enjoy stalking Turkey's abundant wild game, which includes bears, gazelles, boars, deer, pheasant, and quail. Turks are also fond of relaxing at the excellent beaches that are found along the country's thousands of miles of seacoast. During leisure hours, many Turkish men play backgammon, an ancient board game, in local coffeehouses.

A plant that manufactures steel in Eregli, southern Turkey, is part of the nation's recent push to industrialize.

Courtesy of Agency for International Development/Carl Purcell

4) The Economy

In the 1970s Turkey's economy made some impressive strides toward industrial modernization. For example, the Izmir oil refinery began operation, and the huge Keban Dam, built across the upper Euphrates River, generated 6.2 million kilowatt-hours of hydroelectric power. With improvements in farming, Turkey now manages to raise enough food to feed its people. The government is able to influence the development of the economy to a great extent, and this power suggests that there will be increased growth in the future.

Agriculture

Despite a new emphasis on industrialization, however, agriculture is still the mainstay of the Turkish economy. New seeds and farming techniques were introduced during the 1970s and successfully increased crop yields. As a result, Turkey stopped having to import food and became a food exporter. About 95 percent of all Turkish farm families own their own land, and the average farm covers 12 acres. Productivity on some small farms remains low, since landholders are unwilling or unable to introduce modern methods.

World Bank Photo

A combine *(top)* harvests grain in the flat area between Adana and Mersin, while farmers who plant on a smaller scale use slower, more traditional methods *(below)*.

Independent Picture Service

Turkey's varying climates allow the cultivation of a wide array of crops. Anatolian farmers sow wheat and barley in the autumn that ripen the following summer, and apple and cherry trees produce fruit for the fall harvest period.

The chief commercial crops are tobacco and cotton, which are grown in many districts but thrive especially well on the wide plains. Tobacco production is centered in Izmir on the Aegean Sea and Samsun on the Black Sea, and high yields of cotton are found mainly near Adana, a flat southern area ideal for mechanized cultivation.

Dried figs and raisins are produced in the hot western valleys and are exported through the port of Izmir. Apricots and grapes appear in many areas nationwide, and orange trees flourish along the southern coast. Olives come mainly from the mountainous regions to the south, and the annual harvest of nuts—including pistachios, almonds, and hazelnuts—is of national agricultural importance. About half of Turkey's fertile land is being converted to orchards and pasture.

World Bank Photo
A farmer loads a fresh crop of tomatoes that are intended for export into wooden crates.

World Bank Photo
Turkey's agricultural harvest includes a wide variety of fruits and vegetables.

The vast array of Turkey's agriculture is reflected in the bright colors of this Istanbul shopkeeper's stall.

Women of the fertile lands near Rize along the Black Sea bring down bags of tea leaves from the hills to dry in the sun.

A woman and her daughter string together large tobacco leaves, which they will hang in the sun to dry.

Cotton—grown along the coast of the Mediterranean Sea—is among Turkey's leading crops.

Livestock rest on the rocky terrain near Konya in south central Turkey.

Up-to-date machinery helps to extract lignite (rough coal) from the surface at a mine in Elbistan, central Turkey.

Livestock raising fits well into the general farming pattern. Sheep, goats, and cattle are the most profitable animals to raise. The country's population of Angora goats is a natural source of mohair, an expensive cloth or yarn that is silky, fluffy, and strong. Angora is a variation of the name Ankara, and the goats are raised on the central plain south of the capital city.

Mining and Fishing

Turkey holds a rich variety of mineral deposits, yet they remain largely untapped. Lack of funds and a shortage of processing plants have hampered the growth of the nation's potentially valuable mining industry.

The country's most abundant mining resource is coal, which is used for fuel in steel-making plants. The largest coalfield, at Eregli on the Black Sea, is the only substantial deposit in southwestern Asia. Turkey is also one of the world's four principal producers of chromite, from which

The extent of Turkish oil deposits is still being investigated but refineries—such as this one at Batman—continue to process crude oil.

53

chrome is made. The ore comes mostly from the valley near Maras on the nation's southeastern coast. Iron ore is mined at Divrigi, and manganese deposits are exploited near Hopa in the far northeast. Petroleum findings—mainly in the Garzan-Raman field in the upper Tigris River Basin—enable Turkey to produce and refine half of the oil needed to fuel the nation.

Despite its access to three important seas, Turkey has only a modest fishing industry. Based in the Straits, fishermen take advantage of migrations from the Black Sea to the Mediterranean. Anchovies make up the largest part of the catch, which in the 1980s was about 100,000 tons annually.

Manufacturing

Since 1980 Turkey has established an increasingly diverse and sophisticated industrial base, aided by loans from the United States and the International Mon-

Photo by Robert Fried

Vendors display their catch at a fish market in Bursa.

Photo by Robert Fried

Most of Turkey's fishing industry is concentrated in the Straits. Here, fishing boats ply the waters of the Bosporus.

A worker adjusts a machine on the production line of the Rabak copper tubing factory in Istanbul.

At a plant near Bursa, bricks are made in the age-old way. Mud is mixed and poured into molds, after which the pieces are dried in the sun.

etary Fund (IMF). The quality of manufactured goods in Turkey, however, is still far below the level of other countries, even though the nation's exports compete with products from eastern Asia and Europe.

In the 1980s manufacturing in Turkey focused on the food and beverage industries and on the production of textiles that used locally produced cotton. The mill at Kayseri, for example, is the largest textile producer in the Middle East. Most factories are located in and around the large cities of northern and western Turkey.

Iron- and steel-producing plants are concentrated on the coast of the Black Sea. A new steel complex has been opened at the port of Iskenderun on the Mediterranean and has an estimated annual output of two million tons.

One successful aspect of Turkey's economy—that of drug trafficking—has drawn the criticism of Western countries. Turkey used to be one of the primary manufac-

Turkish cotton is spun onto thousands of bobbins at this textile factory.

turers of opium but stopped growing and refining it at the request of the United States beginning in the late 1970s. Turkey, however, still lies between the great opium production centers of Pakistan and Afghanistan and between the large consumption areas of Western Europe and the United States. Despite government attempts to control the traffic, opium gum, morphine base, and heroin are still smuggled through Turkey.

Unemployment

One of the biggest difficulties in recent Turkish history has been unemployment. During the late 1970s, unemployment was among the causes that bred excessive violence, which, in turn, contributed to the 1980 military coup. The unemployment rate in 1985 was 16.7 percent, up from 12.7 percent in 1978.

The unemployment figure would be much higher if not for the more than one

Many skilled Turks leave their homeland to find work in foreign countries, where the wages, benefits, and job opportunities are more attractive.

Shouldering their heavy tools, forestry workers—among the lucky few who are employed by the government—look after an experimental forest.

million Turks who work abroad—mostly in West Germany and Saudi Arabia. Including those who work outside Turkey, the number of employed Turks is roughly 2.3 million. For Turks who work in Europe, the situation is often very difficult. Most foreign workers leave their families at home, and, when Western economies decline, Turkish laborers are the first to be laid off. Although workers sent more than $2.1 billion home to Turkey in 1982, that figure dropped dramatically in 1984. Consequently, the average yearly income per person in the mid-1980s was only $974.

Unemployment affects Turks at all income levels but is especially hard for those at the lower end of the economic scale.

The Keban Dam takes its power from the Firat (Euphrates) River and supplies much of east central Turkey with electricity.

The Bosporus Bridge—the fourth longest suspension bridge in the world—cost $34 million to build.

Energy and Transportation

Although Turkey can produce some oil, its industrial and economic growth still suffers from lack of fossil fuels. About half of the electrical energy generated in the nation comes from hydroelectric plants. The Keban Dam on the upper Euphrates near Elazig has produced power for years, and its output has recently been combined with that of a second dam located downstream from the Keban facility. The government has formulated plans for an even larger project, the Ataturk Dam, to irrigate large farming areas of southwestern Turkey, as well as to supply them with electrical power.

With German aid, the Ottoman sultans built the first Turkish railroads, which connected Istanbul with Paris via the famous Orient Express line. By the time of World War I, railroads linked all parts of the Ottoman Empire to Istanbul and reached other Middle Eastern capitals, such as Baghdad, Cairo, Jerusalem, and Damascus. After independence, a government-owned railway network emerged. Today the Turkish Republic State Railways are perhaps the best in the Middle East, though they do not serve all areas of southeastern and southwestern Turkey.

An excellent highway system, which is now connected to Europe by the Bosporus Bridge, supplements the railways. In the mid-1980s Turkey had almost 40,000 miles of national highways, of which 34,000 were hard-surfaced, all-weather roads. Over a million motor vehicles were registered, including 747,000 cars and 100,000 buses.

Turkish Airlines offers international service from both Istanbul and Ankara, as well as regularly scheduled domestic flights. Istanbul's busy airport handles international traffic, while Ankara is the major center for travel within Turkey.

Istanbul on the Bosporus and Izmir on the Aegean Sea are the main seaports but

New dock facilities at Marmara are designed to ease the shipping traffic at the nearby seaport of Istanbul.

have become increasingly crowded in recent times. Modernizing schemes have upgraded the facilities at Izmir, and a port at Marmara is intended to relieve Istanbul's seaside congestion. Black Sea ports, such as Samsun, Sinop, and Trabzon, have good services but their location means they also attract less traffic.

Tourism

Tourism has developed into a major source of foreign currency for Turkey. In the late 1980s an annual total of about 2.8 million visitors arrived in Turkey and spent an estimated $1.3 billion. Located in the historic Middle East but largely uninvolved in the conflicts of the area, Turkey has been able to increase its share of the tourist market. Since 1984, for example, large numbers of Arabs—from countries such as Saudi Arabia and the United Arab Emirates—have wanted to see the treasures of Islamic Turkey rather than those of Christian Europe. Wealthy, foreign Arabs have

Early Christians—hated and suspected by Roman and Byzantine rulers, as well as by Muslims—hid in the natural rock formations at Cappadocia, near Nevsehir.

Courtesy of Sarah Larson

An ancient slab of stone shows King Mithradates Callinicus *(left)* **clasping the hand of Hercules.**

Courtesy of Cultural and Tourism Office of the Turkish Embassy

Bursa attracts sports enthusiasts to its winter tourism facilities.

even been allowed to buy land in resort areas of Turkey—something Turkish citizens cannot do.

Istanbul's historic buildings, mosques, and art treasures attract thousands of tourists each year. In addition, Turkey's ancient ruins—at Troy, Pergamum, Ephesus, and Cappadocia—bring in interested people from around the world. Moreover, the coastal areas on the Aegean and Mediterranean seas appeal to both Turks and foreign visitors as places to enjoy the warm climate. Ski resorts in the northwest also draw seasonal crowds.

Courtesy of Sarah Larson

Thousands of visitors every year stream through the entrance to Topkapi Palace in Istanbul.

The Hittite settlement at Bogazkoy included a temple complex, royal buildings, and a library. The huge jadelike stone *(right foreground)* may have had a religious use.

Pamukkale—where calcium-rich waters flow down white hillsides into small, shallow pools—is a famous tourist attraction in southwestern Turkey.

Roman architecture abounds throughout Turkey. The Cendere Bridge is still in use 2,000 years after it was built.

Turkish president Kenan Evren helped to return the nation to civilian rule, leading to parliamentary elections in November 1987.

The Future

Turkey in the 1980s is a society faced with difficult choices. As a country with an important historical legacy, it constantly compares past periods of greatness with its problems in the modern era.

The problems that Turkey faces are complex. Twice since 1960, military coups have toppled the government. Confronted with enormous economic difficulties, Turkish politicians must always be alert to widespread economic crises and to the social problems that usually follow. This threat of instability, in turn, places great stress on the political system and jeopardizes the democratic form of government that the Turks hope to maintain. Moreover, tensions between Greeks and Turks continue, and conflict in the Aegean or in Cyprus is always a possibility. Thus, despite a magnificent past, Turkey's recent economic and domestic troubles force Turks to view the nation's future with cautious optimism.

Index

Adrianople, 14, 24
Aegean Sea, 5, 7, 9–12, 17, 19, 50, 59, 61, 63
Agriculture, 8–10, 12–13, 17, 35, 48–53, 59. *See also* Cotton; Fruit; Livestock; Tobacco
Air transportation, 59
Alexander III (the Great), 20
Allies, 30–32
Anatolia (Asia Minor), 7–10, 12–14, 18–22, 24–25, 30, 32, 40, 50
Ancient kingdoms, 17–21
Ankara, 6, 15–17, 31, 34, 45, 53, 59
Arabs, 21–22, 25, 30, 36, 60–61
Ararat, Mount, 9
Archaeology, 5, 17–18
Architecture, 2, 5–7, 14, 16–17, 24, 36–37
Armed conflicts, 6, 19–21, 24–33, 63
  between Turkey and Cyprus, 33
  civil war, 30–32
  Janissary Corps, 26–28
  military coups d'état, 6, 33, 63
  wars with Russia, 29
Armenians, 30–31, 36
Arts, 36–39, 44, 61. *See also* Miniatures
Asia, 5–7, 22, 25, 35–36, 53
Asia Minor. *See* Anatolia
Assyrian Empire, 18–19
Ataturk, Mustafa Kemal, 6, 14–15, 29–32, 44
Balkans, 21, 24, 26
Black Sea, 7, 9–10, 13, 50–51, 53–55, 60
Bosporus, 7, 10–11, 15, 20, 54
Bosporus Bridge, 10, 59
Bridges, 10, 14–15, 59, 63. *See also* Bosporus Bridge; Galata Bridge
Bulgaria, 7, 10, 24–25
Bursa, 13–14, 24, 46, 54–55, 61
Byzantine Empire, 5, 20–22, 25, 36, 60
Byzantium, 20. *See also* Constantinople; Istanbul
Carvings and sculpture, 5, 19, 37, 44, 61
Central Plateau, 8–9, 12–13
Central Powers, 29–30
Christianity, 21, 24–25, 30, 36–37, 60
Cities and towns, 2, 12, 14–17
Climate, 12, 50
Clothing, 3, 41
Constantine I, 5, 20–21
Constantinople, 5, 14, 20–21, 25, 36. *See also* Byzantium; Istanbul
Constitution, 32, 34
Cotton, 50, 52, 55–56
Crafts, 38–39, 44
Crimean War, 29
Cyprus, 29, 33, 63
Dardanelles, 7, 10–11, 20, 24
Democracy, 6, 32–34, 63
Drug trafficking, 55–56
Economy, 6, 48–63
Education, 43–45
Egypt, 18, 21
Elections, 6, 33–34
Employment, 6, 56–57
Energy, 11, 48, 58–59

Ephesus (ruins), 17, 19, 61
Ertugrul, 22
Ethnic groups, 35–36
Euphrates River, 11, 48, 58–59
Europe, 5–7, 9–10, 14, 22, 24–25, 28–31, 56–57, 59–60
Evren, Kenan, 33, 63
Exports, 48, 50, 55
Fishing, 54
Flora and fauna, 12–14, 47
Food, 46–47
Forestry, 57
Forests, 8, 13
France, 29–30
Fruit, 9, 17, 50
Galata Bridge, 15, 22
Gallipoli campaign, 30
Gallipoli Peninsula, 9, 11, 24, 29
Golden Horn, 15, 22
Government, 6, 15, 25–28, 32–34, 43–46, 55–57, 63
  and drug trafficking, 55–56
  during Ottoman Empire, 25–28
  and education, 43–45
  and health, 15, 45–46
  structure of, 34
Grand National Assembly, 31, 34
Great Britain, 29–30, 33
Greece, 5, 7, 17, 19–21, 29–31, 33, 35, 38–39, 63
Hagia Sophia, 17, 24–25, 36–37
Health, 15, 45–46
History, 5–6, 14–15, 18–34
  early empires, 18–22
  modern era, 33–34
  Ottoman Empire, 22–32
  post-World War II, 33
  republic established, 32
Hittite Empire, 5, 17–19, 35, 62
Hittites, 17–19, 35, 62
Hydroelectric power, 11, 48, 58–59
Industry, 48, 53–61
Inonu, Ismet, 33
International Monetary Fund, 54–55
Iran, 7, 30, 34
Iraq, 7, 11, 30, 34
Islam, 21–22, 25–28, 32, 34, 36–41, 43–44, 60. *See also* Muslims
Istanbul, 7, 10–11, 14–17, 22, 25–26, 28, 37, 47, 51, 55, 59–61. *See also* Byzantium; Constantinople
Istranca Mountains, 9
Izmir, 13, 17, 30, 48, 50, 59–60. *See also* Smyrna
Izmit Valley, 9
Janissary Corps, 26–28
Judicial system, 27–28, 32, 34, 41, 43
Keban Dam, 48, 58
Kemal, Mustafa. *See* Ataturk, Mustafa Kemal
Konya, 18, 37, 52
Koran, 26, 28, 43–44
Kurdistan, 30–31, 34, 39. *See also* Kurds
Kurds, 35–36
Lakes, 9. *See also* Tuz Lake; Van, Lake
Language, 38–39, 43
Latin Empire, 21
Legislature, 34
Literacy, 43–45

Literature, 39–40
Livestock, 52–53
Manufacturing, 48, 54–56
Maps and charts, 4, 8, 28, 42
Marmara (island), 60
Marmara, Sea of, 7, 10–11
Mediterranean Sea, 7, 9–10, 12, 21, 29, 52, 54, 61
Middle East, 11, 14, 21–22, 25, 28–29, 44, 55, 59–60
Military, 6, 33–34
Minerals, 53–54
Miniatures, 22–23, 27, 38
Mining, 53–54
Mosques, 6, 17, 25, 36–37, 41, 61
Mountains, 8–9, 12–13
Muslims, 5, 25, 27, 32, 39–41, 43–44, 60. *See also* Islam
Nationalist movement, 17, 31, 39–40
Natural resources, 8, 13, 53–54
North Africa, 21–22, 28–29
Ottoman Empire, 2, 6, 14, 22–32, 34, 36–39, 43, 59
Ottoman Turks, 5–6, 17, 22–32, 36–38, 59
People, 6, 15, 25, 32, 35–47, 56–57
  employment, 6, 56–57
  ethnic groups, 35–36
  income per capita, 57
  standard of living, 15, 35, 45–46, 56–57
  women, 6, 25, 32, 41–43, 45
Pergamum (ruins), 17, 61
Persia, 5, 19–20, 35, 39
Persian Empire, 19–20, 35
Persian Gulf, 11
Political activism, 26–27, 33–34
Political parties, 33
Population, 6, 15, 35, 44
Ports, 10–11, 59–60
Poverty, 15
Presidents, 31–34, 63
Provinces, 34
Railways, 59
Rainfall, 12
Religion, 25–28, 32, 34, 40–41, 43–44. *See also* Christianity; Islam; Muslims
  sultans' religious power, 25–27
Religious buildings, 5–6, 19, 21, 24, 37, 41, 62
Religious crusades, 21
Rivers, 11–12. *See also* Euphrates River; Tigris River
Rize, 9, 51
Roads, highways, 2, 9, 59
Roman Empire, 20–21, 63
Romania, 10, 24, 29
Ruins, 5, 17–19, 61–63
Rural life, 35–36, 40, 44–45
Saudi Arabia, 57, 60
Seljuk Turks, 5, 22, 35–36, 38
Serbia, 24, 29
Sèvres, Treaty of, 30–32
Shatt-al-Arab, 11
Slavery, 26
Smali Andalou Mountains, 9
Smyrna, 17, 30. *See also* Izmir
Soviet Union, 7–8, 10, 12, 29, 31, 38
Sports and recreation, 12, 47, 61
Standard of living, 15, 35, 45–46, 56–57
Straits, the, 7, 10, 15, 29–32, 54
Sultans, 6, 16, 23–29, 36, 39, 59

Syria, 7, 9, 11, 18, 21, 30
Taurus Mountains, 9
Textiles, 53, 55–56
Thrace, 7, 9–10, 20, 30, 32
Tigris River, 11, 54
Tobacco, 50, 52
Topkapi Palace, 16–17, 26, 36, 61
Topography, 7–12, 60
Tourism, 60–62
Trade, 10, 17, 19
Transportation, 11, 59–60
Troy, 5, 9, 19, 61
Turkey
  birth of the republic, 32–33
  boundaries, size, and location of, 7–10
  flag of, 34
  future outlook of, 63
  population of, 35
"Turkish Riviera," 12
Turks, 5, 22, 25, 29–33, 35
Tuz Lake, 9
Unemployment, 6, 56–57
United Nations, 33
United States, 33, 54, 56
Universities, 44–45
Van, Lake, 9
Westernization, 6, 28, 32, 39, 41, 43–44, 48
West Germany, 57
Women, 6, 25, 32, 41–43, 45
World War I, 14, 29–30, 59
World War II, 32–33
Writers and poets, 40
Young Turks, 29